THE BEST OF

MAC 2013

Cartoons from the *Daily Mail*

Stan McMurtry **mac**

Edited by Mark Bryant

PORTICO

For my pal from childhood, Glyn, and his wife Annette

First published in the United Kingdom in 2013 by
Portico Books
10 Southcombe Street
London
W14 0RA

An imprint of Anova Books Company Ltd

ISBN 9781909396012

A CIP catalogue record for this book is available from the British Library.

10 9 8 7 6 5 4 3 2 1

Printed and bound by Bookwell, Finland.

This book can be ordered direct from the publisher at
www.anovabooks.com

Preface

2013. Walk down any street in the UK and easily recognisable amongst its teeming masses is a body of people whose careworn, anxious faces, furrowed brows, stooped shoulders and haggard expressions give away the profession they have chosen to follow. Yes, spare a thought for the Cartoonists of Britain whose job it is in these days of gloom and austerity to rise from their beds, clutch their pens with nibbled fingers and try valiantly to bring a modicum of cheer to our downtrodden citizens suffering from dip and double-dip recession.

I know your heart bleeds, but wipe away that tear. Hopefully the following pages will cheer you up as you look back on some of the newsworthy events of the year. However, if things are really bad, you can always hang the book up by one corner in the loo. Uncomfortable, but it'll save a few bob.

Mac

There were accusations of drug-taking in the women's swimming final at the London Olympics when 16-year-old Ye Shiwen from China won gold medals in the 200 and 400 metres individual medley races in record-breaking times.

'Who needs drugs? It's all down to hard work and our training methods.' *1 August 2012*

Britain's women's football team beat Brazil, silver medallists at the Beijing and Athens Olympics, to gain a place in the quarter-finals.

'It's Mrs Warburton from up the road. Do you fancy a kick-about in the park?' *2 August*

The popularity of cycling in Britain soared when Bradley Wiggins took gold in the time-trial event to bring his tally of Olympic medals (won in Sydney, Athens, Beijing and London) to seven, making him the most decorated British Olympian ever.

'A curse on Bradley Wiggins!' *3 August*

Britain's successes at the Olympics continued to enthral the public with further gold medals in tennis, sailing, the heptathlon, long jump and 10,000 metres. Meanwhile, NASA scientists celebrated the successful landing of the Curiosity rover vehicle on the surface of Mars.

'The first pictures are in, Hank.' *7 August*

As Britain won its first showjumping gold medal since the Helsinki Olympics in 1952, 36-year-old Sir Chris Hoy took his sixth gold medal for cycling.

'He was perfectly happy with his gold medal for showjumping until he saw Sir Chris Hoy.' *8 August*

Swimming superstar Michael Phelps, who had recently won his eighteenth gold medal for the USA, confessed to urinating in the pool during competitions, saying that it was normal if a swimmer was in the water for long periods of time.

'Bernard! Michael Phelps meant it's normal for SWIMMERS to pee in the pool!' *9 August*

Britain's Nicola Adams became the first woman boxer ever to win an Olympic title when she beat China's Cancan Ren – the world's number one – to take gold and become flyweight boxing champion in this newly admitted Olympic event.

'I'm home, darling. Got any plans for the evening?' *10 August*

Mo Farah became the first Briton ever to win Olympic gold in the 5,000 and 10,000 metres and celebrated with his trademark 'Mo-bot' hands-on-head gesture. Jamaican gold-medal sprinter Usain Bolt celebrated his own wins with a pointing-hands stance.

'Next!' *14 August*

Research funded by the British Heart Foundation revealed that people in their fifties could reduce the risk of heart attack by gentle exercise such as gardening, DIY and brisk walking. Meanwhile, a Suffolk couple won more than £148 million in the EuroMillions lottery.

'Setting a good example, my foot. *You'd* do that if you'd just won 148 million quid.' *15 August*

The Department of Health announced that it planned to toughen up the rules regulating cosmetic surgery clinics to protect women from botched operations administered by poorly-trained staff.

'After all the recent horror stories, I wasn't going to let any poorly-trained cosmetic cowboy do your liposuction.' *16 August*

WikiLeaks fugitive, Julian Assange, who had claimed asylum in the Embassy of Ecuador in London to escape extradition to Sweden on sex assault charges, addressed the media from the embassy's balcony.

'Julian, Julian. Wherefore art thou, Julian?' *21 August*

Prince Harry hit the headlines when mobile phone pictures were published on the internet showing him playing strip billiards and cavorting naked with women in a swimming pool at a hotel in Las Vegas.

'Come on, fantasise! You're Prince Harry and you've just chased me into the swimming pool...' *24 August*

Fifty-two-year-old Prince Andrew, Duke of York, was one of a 40-member team that abseiled down Europe's tallest building, the recently opened 1,017-foot-high London Bridge Tower ('The Shard'), to raise money for charity.

'Oi! I hope you royals aren't going to make a habit of this. I've just washed that bit!' *4 September*

When a couple from his Leicestershire constituency were arrested for shooting four men who raided their home, International Development Minister Alan Duncan said 'justice should support them and prosecute the burglars' and called for a change in the law.

'When did you first notice that one of the garden gnomes was missing?' *5 September*

London Mayor Boris Johnson accused the Government of making preparations to break its pledge to block a third runway at Heathrow Airport when anti-runway Transport Secretary, Justine Greening, was moved from her job in a Cabinet reshuffle.

'Looks like they've made a decision, Boris...' *6 September*

A judge at Teesside Crown Court praised burglars for their courage, claimed prison 'very rarely does anybody any good' and allowed a serial offender to walk free with a suspended sentence.

'I've always longed to do something brave and courageous. So would you mind awfully telling me where you keep the silver?' *7 September*

At the Labour Party Conference in Manchester, Shadow Chancellor Ed Balls pledged to spend the estimated £3 billion proceeds from the forthcoming 4G mobile phone spectrum sale on building 100,000 affordable homes.

'That's right. We're converts to the Ed Balls fiscal policy. After this meal and a shopping spree, we're goin' to build 100,000 affordable new 'omes.' *2 October*

A scandal broke over allegations that the BBC had tried to cover up knowledge that the disc jockey and TV star, Sir Jimmy Savile, had abused girls and young women. Meanwhile, the *Sunday Mirror* published an interview with the son of Lord Lucan, the peer who disappeared in 1974 after allegedly killing his children's nanny.

'Till this Jimmy Savile scandal blows over, the board thinks you should lie low for a while, Lord Lucan.' *3 October*

At the Conservative Party Conference in Birmingham, the Chancellor George Osborne and Work and Pensions Secretary Iain Duncan Smith unveiled plans for a 'welfare revolution' which included cutting benefits for those who chose to have additional children while unemployed.

'Surprise, surprise, Mum and Dad. Your little boy has come back home.' *9 October*

Police in Lancashire fired a 50,000-volt Taser stun-gun at a blind man, mistaking his white stick for a samurai sword. Meanwhile, Government Chief Whip Andrew Mitchell denied swearing at officers who had refused to open the main gates of Downing Street to allow him to exit on his bicycle.

'Right, lads. Here comes Andrew Mitchell now and – oh my goodness! Isn't that a samurai sword he's carrying?' *19 October*

In a new drive to cut crime and reoffending, David Cameron unveiled plans to introduce a 'payment by results' scheme, in which those parts of the Probation Service dealing with rehabilitation would be outsourced to private-sector security firms.

'Mr Wilkins' company is taking care of your rehabilitation, Wayne. If you don't behave you get cemented into a flyover on the M4.' *23 October*

Lawyers acting for the numerous alleged victims of abuse by Sir Jimmy Savile prepared to sue the BBC for millions of pounds in compensation.

'I see. You were just a vulnerable girl of 69 when he drove up in his Rolls and climbed into your cardboard box where the incident took place?' *24 October*

At a special reception at Buckingham Palace held by the Queen to honour Britain's Olympic and Paralympic stars, judo silver medallist Gemma Gibbons used her mobile phone to take a picture of one of the visitors' toilets and tweeted it to her followers.

'Lock the door after you. Some b******'s taken photographs of the visitors' loo!' *26 October*

After an outbreak of the deadly fungal disease 'ash dieback', which threatened to repeat the devastation of Dutch Elm Disease, the Government took drastic measures, burning 100,000 infected ash trees and banning their import from overseas.

'Don't you worry, sir. I've had a good look at your ash trees and there's no sign of any spreading fungal diseases.' *30 October*

David Cameron and Scotland's First Minister, Alex Salmond, signed the Edinburgh Agreement promising a referendum on Scottish independence from the UK in 2014. Meanwhile, the Government announced contracts worth £350 million, and thousands of Scottish jobs, to build a new generation of Trident submarines for the UK.

'Thought we'd let you know, Mr Salmond. Your man canvassing for Scottish independence is just leaving...' *31 October*

There seemed to be a rift in the Government's view on the future of wind farms when newly appointed Conservative Energy Minister John Hayes said that Britain had had enough of them in contrast to the official view held by LibDem Energy Secretary Ed Davey.

'Aye, lad. Losing our elms and then our ash trees was bad enough, but then the great wind-turbine blight started in 2012...' *1 November*

In one of the closest presidential elections in US history, Democrat Barack Obama and Republican Mitt Romney were neck and neck in the polls. Meanwhile, Superstorm Sandy battered the east coast of the USA, bringing widespread devastation and leaving millions without homes.

'Shucks, Mary Lou. We've been here over a week now. Did you have to say, "Get lost, Buster. We're voting Obama?" ' *6 November*

Conservative Chief Whip Sir George Young suspended Nadine Dorries, Tory MP for Mid Bedfordshire, when it was revealed that she had flown to Australia to take part in ITV's *I'm a Celebrity...Get Me Out of Here* and would be away from Parliament for up to a month.

'It's the Chief Whip's Office for you, Nadine. I think it may be bad news.' *7 November*

After one of the most expensive and most bitterly fought US presidential elections ever, the Democratic Party's Barack Obama was returned to the White House for four more years.

'It's Clancy's furniture removals. There was nobody in when they called so they've left it on the White House lawn.' *8 November*

The Rt Rev. Justin Welby, the Eton- and Cambridge-educated Bishop of Durham, and a former oil industry executive, was appointed the new Archbishop of Canterbury.

'It was a stitch-up, lads. All that trouble I had nicking the gear and I didn't even get a bleedin' interview!' *9 November*

Lord Patten, Chairman of the BBC Trust, faced calls for his resignation after admitting that he had been aware of the plan for a BBC2's *Newsnight* programme to imply (falsely) that former Tory treasurer Lord McAlpine – a grandson of the founder of the McAlpine construction company – had been involved with child abuse.

'Some of Lord McAlpine's relatives are here to see you, sir...' *13 November*

At the Conservative Party conference in Birmingham Chancellor George Osborne announced a further £10 billion in welfare cuts to combat benefit fraudsters and the 'work shy'. Meanwhile, 'hate preacher' Abu Qatada was released on bail to live on state benefits with his family in London.

'Donald, do we need some light dusting done about the house?' *14 November*

After US General David Petraeus, head of the CIA, resigned over a sex scandal, it emerged that General John Allen, nominated as NATO's Supreme Allied Commander in Europe, had also been involved with one of the women in the case while stationed at the US Army's Central Command in Tampa, Florida.

'Godammit, soldier. In this man's army you salute when a general passes by!' *15 November*

As the Government unveiled new regulations to curb residents' rights to protest against plans for airports, railways and roads it was revealed that the Chancellor's Autumn Statement would include a 'mansion tax by the back door' by raising stamp duty on properties worth more than £1 million.

'Look on the bright side, dear. We probably won't ever have to pay a mansion tax now.' *20 November*

The General Synod of the Church of England voted by a narrow margin against the introduction of women bishops.

'Oh, you're back, Mrs Scroggins? I thought you were going to have a late career move.' *21 November*

Prime Minister David Cameron called for the General Synod to think again about the rejection of women bishops as many felt that the vote against them would lead to the Church losing its credibility with the public.

'My sermon today asks the question: could the vote against women bishops diminish the Church's credibility with the public?' *22 November*

Lord Hall of Birkenhead, head of the Royal Opera House and a former director of BBC News, was appointed BBC Director-General.

'I preferred it when Fiona Bruce just read the news.' *23 November*

Labour-run Rotherham Borough Council removed three children from their foster parents because they were members of the UK Independence Party. Meanwhile, days of torrential rain plunged Britain's transport network into chaos.

'Did you have to tell them we're with UKIP?' *28 November*

Speaking on BBC2's *Newsnight*, Planning Minister Nick Boles announced that up to 2 million acres of green fields, an area the size of Devon, may have to be sacrificed to solve the housing problem.

'Move over, love. I've got some bad news.' *29 November*

Lord Justice Leveson's report on the future of press regulation in the wake of the phone-hacking scandal recommended tough new legislation and the formation of an independent watchdog with the power to issue fines of up to £1 million.

'Looks like the new press regulatory body has started work already.' *30 November*

In an attempt to cut the British Army's electricity and gas bills, its 110,000 military and civilian personnel were ordered to work from home for 25 days over the Christmas holiday period.

'Don't shoot! We're only here to sing a few carols!' *4 December*

Buckingham Palace announced that the Duke and Duchess of Cambridge were expecting their first child.

'Remind me again, dear. Is it knit one, purl one or knit two, purl four?' *5 December*

In his Autumn Statement, Chancellor George Osborne announced a £5 billion investment in roads and schools, funded by taxes on higher earners' pensions and high-street banks and a capping of the benefits system.

'It's George Osborne on the phone – release the tax inspectors!' *6 December*

After spending three nights in the King Edward VII Hospital in London suffering from acute morning sickness the Duchess of Cambridge returned home.

'Surprise, surprise, Kate, darling. A welcome-home breakfast – champagne, porridge, bacon and eggs, kippers...' *7 December*

Though Britain faced a triple-dip recession and there were rumours of chemical weapons being used in the civil war in Syria, Parliament's main concern seemed to be with the proposed new legislation to allow gay marriages.

'Thank heavens today we won't be wasting time discussing trivia like the economy or Syria.' *11 December*

As temperatures in Britain plummeted, *Channel 4 News* revealed the new craze for 'sexting' in which boys and girls as young as 13 sent each other intimate photos on their mobile phones as a dating aid.

'Another one sexting, sarge. Chuck him in the back with the others.' *12 December*

Amidst stormy debate in the House of Commons, Culture Secretary Maria Miller vowed to fast-track plans to legalise gay marriage by 2014, though the Church of England would be exempted.

'We've been invited to a wedding – who the hell are Hotlips and Bunnykins?' *13 December*

Energy Secretary Ed Davey gave the go-ahead for a new phase of drilling for UK-based 'shale gas' released by the controversial process of 'fracking', which involves pumping water and chemicals into underground shale deposits at high pressure, in order to release trapped pockets of natural gas.

'Good news, George. Apparently our gas bills might be a few pence cheaper.' *14 December*

Deputy Prime Minister Nick Clegg renewed his call to stop winter fuel allowances and other benefits for well-off pensioners. Meanwhile, 76-year-old former Italian premier Silvio Berlusconi – famed for his 'bunga-bunga' sex parties – announced that he would run for a fourth term in office.

'If we do lose our winter fuel allowance, Godfrey is keen to have the Berlusconi heating system installed in his room, whatever that is.' *18 December*

To mark her Diamond Jubilee, David Cameron invited the Queen to attend a Cabinet meeting at 10 Downing Street for the first time in her 60-year reign. By doing so she became the first monarch since George III (in 1781) to sit in on a regular Cabinet meeting.

'Would you mind calling another Cabinet meeting? The Queen thinks it'll do wonders for my insomnia.' *19 December*

According to the Ancient Mayans the world was due to end on 22 December 2012. Asked by the *Daily Mail* what she would do if it was her last day on earth, former Tory MP Edwina Currie said 'I would find George Clooney and spend the day with him.'

'Well honestly! I bet he won't be nipping out to the service station to buy her Christmas presents!' *21 December*

Britons nationwide celebrated the New Year.

'... and guess what, mother? Bernard is sticking to his resolution – it's nearly 12 hours since he touched a cigarette.' *1 January 2013*

In yet another shake-up of the welfare system, the Government announced that child benefit would no longer be paid to those households in which one parent earns £60,000 or more, and those households where one parent earns £50–60,000 would have their child benefit cut.

'Wonderful news. My boss has given me a reduction in pay.' *8 January*

It was revealed that lethal stun-guns capable of discharging up to a million volts (20 times more powerful than British police Tasers) could be bought openly online and were being illegally imported into the UK.

'I know what you're thinking – Christmas is over, when is she going home? So okay, punk, make my day. Ask the question!' *9 January*

Justice Secretary Chris Grayling announced plans to build Britain's biggest prison, capable of housing 2,000 inmates, and to close five of the country's older jails.

'Twenty-five years I've spent on that tunnel!' *11 January*

A report by the All-Party Parliamentary Group for Drug Policy Reform recommended that the possession and use of Class A drugs such as heroin, ecstasy and crack cocaine should be decriminalised, and also called for licences to be issued to allow drug-dealers to sell co-called 'legal highs'.

'... and what's more, it's not just my opinion that "legal highs" should be freely available.
Ask my team: Pinky the elephant and Bruno our one-legged rhino...' *15 January*

A 61-year-old Christian British Airways check-in clerk won her six-year battle to wear a cross at work after the European Court of Human Rights in Strasbourg judged in her favour.

'Don't push your luck, Sharon!' *16 January*

DNA tests by the Food Safety Authority of Ireland discovered that beefburgers sold by Tesco and three other supermarket chains, and distributed to their shops throughout the UK, contained horsemeat.

'HE'S BEHIND YOU! – The Tesco burger man.' *17 January*

The Big Freeze hit Britain with temperatures as low as minus 13 degrees Celsius in some areas. Meanwhile, a new film adaptation of Victor Hugo's 1862 novel, *Les Misérables*, starring Hugh Jackman and Helena Bonham Carter, became a box-office smash.

'I thought this is what you wanted to see – Les Miserables.' *22 January*

In an interview to mark the end of his four-month tour of duty as an attack helicopter pilot in Afghanistan, Prince Harry – still dogged by reports of his naked escapades in Las Vegas – admitted that he had personally been responsible for the deaths of a number of insurgents.

'Given your remarks on the Taliban, Harry, I suppose a game of strip billiards is out of the question?' *23 January*

In a tough public statement David Cameron issued a historic ultimatum to Brussels and pledged that there would be a referendum on Britain's membership of the EU by 2017. Meanwhile, a man was cleared of assault for whipping his lover with a rope in a sex game inspired by E.L. James's bestselling novel *Fifty Shades of Grey*.

Fifty Shades of Dave *24 January*

It was revealed that local councils in some parts of Britain were using security firms employing ex-servicemen to collect litter fines on commission, with 64,000 tickets being issued in England in 2012 compared with just 727 in 1997.

'Think hard, George. When you put the cat out did you drop a toffee wrapper?' *30 January*

There were strong objections by the Association of Chief Police Officers when the Home Office suggested relaxing the rules of employment to allow foreign police chiefs from countries such as the USA, Canada, Australia and New Zealand to serve in the UK.

'Okay, guys. Listen up. The Brits want me to kick ass over in the UK – but don't worry, it's a reciprocal arrangement...' *31 January*

To mark the 150th anniversary of the London Underground, Prince Charles and the Duchess of Cornwall travelled from Farringdon to King's Cross (one stop) on the Metropolitan Line.

'I don't understand. Charles and Camilla said it was quite jolly.' *1 February*

The House of Commons vote on gay marriage was passed by a large majority with 400 MPs in favour and 175 against. However, more than half of Conservative MPs voted against it.

'Don't raise your hopes, Norman. I've got a feeling that Brad Pitt is already spoken for.' *6 February*

In a damning report, Robert Francis QC revealed that 1,200 patients had died from neglect at Stafford Hospital between 2005 and 2008, and thousands of others had been subjected to inhumane and degrading treatment. Meanwhile, it was reported that more than 180 Britons had opted for 'assisted suicide' at the Dignitas clinic in Switzerland.

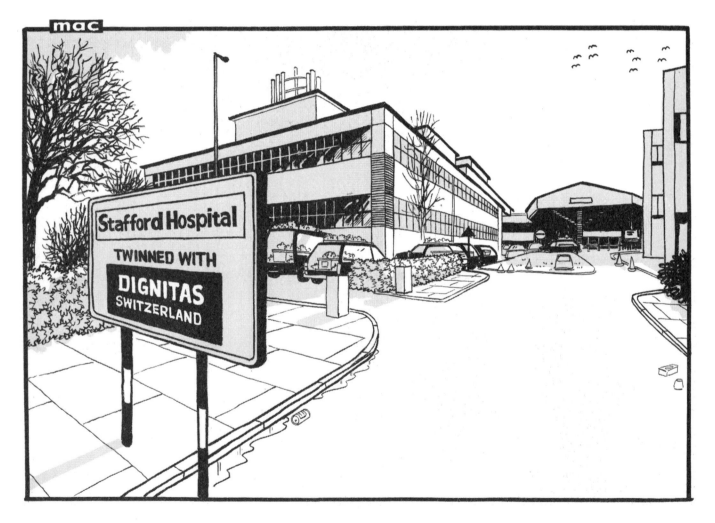

7 February

As the winter weather worsened, a new TV advertisement for fashion chain H&M showed the 37-year-old footballer David Beckham running through the streets of Hollywood in just his underpants.

'That's right, Mrs Beckham. Your husband's out in his underpants again... okay, we'll shove him on the roof rack.' *8 February*

After the shock resignation of Pope Benedict XVI, the first pontiff to step down from the post in 600 years, there was speculation about his successor. Meanwhile, former Prime Minister Tony Blair was one of many celebrity guests at Sir David Tang's Chinese New Year party held at the Dorchester Hotel.

'He's right, you know – we've never had a Pope Tony.' *12 February*

As the mislabelled horsemeat scandal grew, it was discovered that the source of the contaminated products was an abattoir in Romania. Meanwhile, there were fears that huge numbers of illegal immigrants would arrive in Britain as Romania prepared to join the EU's passport-free travel zone.

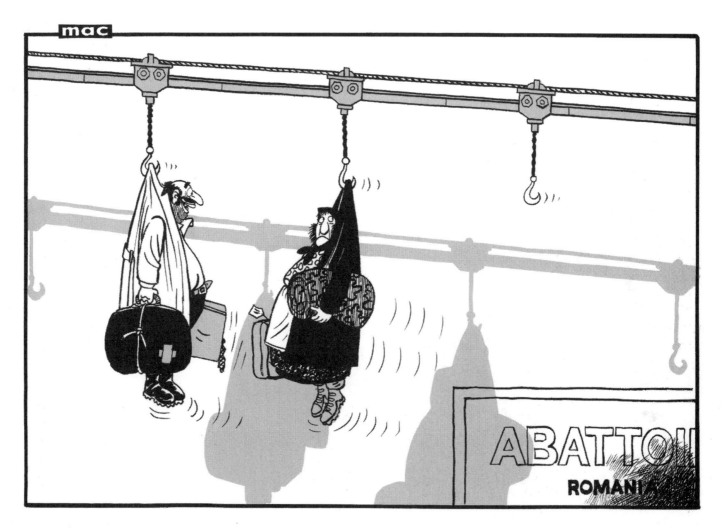

'... so I said, "If you can smuggle horse into the UK, you can smuggle us in." "Okay," he said, "Twenty smackers." ' *13 February*

The horsemeat crisis took another turn when police raids in Yorkshire and West Wales revealed that meat from British horses had also been found in takeaway burgers and kebabs.

'I believe the police are checking the local abattoirs.' *14 February*

In a further twist to the meat-labelling scandal it was discovered that frozen pork meatballs sold by the Swedish company IKEA had contained horsemeat.

'Well it says "pork" on the label.' *15 February*

There was more criticism of NHS chiefs when an NHS whistleblower, sacked in 2010, defied a gagging order to break his silence about a care scandal at the United Lincolnshire Hospital Trust that may have costs the lives of 670 patients since 2009.

'Blow no whistles, see no whistles, hear no whistles.' *19 February*

In a lecture at the British Museum, Booker Prize-winning novelist Hilary Mantel described the Duchess of Cambridge as having 'a perfect plastic smile', appeared to have been 'designed by a committee' and was 'a shop-window mannequin with no personality of her own'.

'Mirror, mirror on the wall, who is the fairest of them all?... OH B*******!' *20 February*

A 37-year-old mother of eleven, living on benefits in Gloucestershire, was reported to own a horse and was about to move into a newly-built £400,000, six-bedroom, three-bathroom, energy-saving house at the taxpayers' expense.

'I'm sorry. The lady of the house will make no further comment about her eleven children, the new six-bedroomed abode being built or her horse.' *21 February*

The jury in the trial of Chris Huhne's ex-wife Vicky Pryce, accused of perverting the course of justice by accepting his speeding points, was discharged by the judge as the questions they raised showed that they had failed to understand the case and were 'highly unlikely' to reach a verdict.

'One more question, m'lud – does a full house beat a royal flush?' *22 February*

In the run-up to the by-election in Chris Huhne's former constituency of Eastleigh in Hampshire, the LibDem leader, Nick Clegg, was accused of a cover-up after admitting he had known that the party's former Chief Executive, Lord Rennard, had faced claims of molesting women.

'Okay, which is it? Are you here for a grope or to ask me to take on your speeding penalty points?' *26 February*

Despite a massive 15 percent surge in profits by Centrica, the owners of British Gas, and huge bonuses for its top executives, the company planned new gas price rises for its 12 million customers.

'It's endlessly fascinating. From up here one can see the strained, worried faces of mere mortals as they struggle to pay their gas bills.' *28 February*

Environment Secretary Owen Paterson announced that thousands of badgers would be culled in the summer to limit the spread of tuberculosis in cattle. Meanwhile, bankers continued to pocket huge bonuses as savings interest rates hit at an all-time low.

'Humans are so stupid – the country would be a lot healthier if they had a cull of bankers.' *1 March*

The Queen, aged 86, was admitted into hospital with a stomach bug.

'Listen... the national anthem... she must be leaving! – EVERYBODY UP!' *5 March*

An unknown man, dressed as Batman, escorted a wanted criminal into a police station in Bradford, handed him over to the duty officer, and then left.

'I was on my way out to rid the city of crime and corruption, but next door's cat got me on the landing.' *6 March*

Questioned by a Health Select Committee, the Chief Executive of the NHS, Sir David Nicholson, claimed he had no knowledge of the care scandal at Stafford Hospital or of gagging orders imposed on hospital staff over high death rates.

'Makes you wonder, doesn't it? We're in here, he's out there.' *7 March*

A study published in *BMC Medicine* found that food containing processed meat, such as sausages and burgers, could cause cancer and heart disease. Meanwhile, environmental experts called for a huge cull of deer to stop damage to woodlands, wildflowers and crops.

'Honestly, Daphne. I was happy to take my chances with the processed meat in sausages...' *8 March*

At Southwark Crown Court former LibDem MP Chris Huhne and his ex-wife Vicky Pryce were each sentenced to eight months in prison for perverting the course of justice over their plot to swap driving penalty points.

'I love this bit – it's where he asks her to take on his speeding penalty points.' *12 March*

Britain was plunged into its worst spring freeze for 27 years with blizzards sweeping the country and the wind-chill factor driving temperatures down to minus 12 degrees Celsius.

'I've just heard the first cuckoo of spring – he was hammering on the door to come in.' *13 March*

A 62-year-old man from Merthyr Tydfil, South Wales, supposedly on sick leave, was sacked from his job when television news footage showed him wrestling with a six-foot shark to keep children safe on a beach in Queensland, Australia.

'For heaven's sake, Dennis. Put it back! You're supposed to be on sick leave!' *14 March*

Seventy-six-year-old Cardinal Mario Bergoglio of Buenos Aires, a known supporter of Argentina's claim to the Falklands Islands, was elected the new pope. Taking the name of Francis I, he became the first non-European pope in 1,300 years.

'Well we've never had a plague of locusts or pestilence before.' *15 March*

Thousands of Britons living in Cyprus suffered along with the rest of the country's citizens when the EU imposed a bank tax on savers – resulting in frozen accounts and closed ATMs – as a condition of the £8.7 billion rescue package to save its economy.

'No need for guns, lads. Just tell them you're from the EU.' *19 March*

A new press regulation charter was agreed between MPs and members of the pro-regulation pressure group Hacked Off, fronted by the actor Hugh Grant.

'It's Hugh Grant on the phone. He wants tomorrow's headline changed, a rewrite of Page 4 and the film critic castrated.' *20 March*

In his Budget Chancellor George Osborne unveiled a new £130 billion 'Help to Buy' scheme, which will give interest-free loans for five years to first-time buyers to top up the deposits required to purchase newly-built properties.

'For heaven's sake, Bernard. He's only 12!' *21 March*

The Budget also announced that working parents would be able to claim back 20 percent of their nursery, childminder or nanny costs up to a total of £1,200 per child, but that those parents who chose to stay at home with their children would receive no benefits.

'Miss Jones. Call building maintenance. I keep hearing slurping noises.' *22 March*

As preparations were made at St Paul's Cathedral for the funeral of former Prime Minister Margaret Thatcher, inhabitants of the Falklands Islands supported a proposal to rename Port Stanley, their capital, as Port Margaret in her honour.

'Once we get there, does anyone know the way to St Paul's?' *11 April*

Further details emerged of the arrangements for the funeral of the Iron Lady. Meanwhile, new figures from the NHS Organ Donor Register revealed that the number of Britons donating their organs after death had risen by 50 percent since 2008.

'If only she could've donated a fraction of her guts and determination to today's politicians.' *12 April*

The BBC were accused of using ten British students from the London School of Economics as a 'human shield' when they were accompanied on an eight-day trip to North Korea by a *Panorama* team filming a secret documentary inside the country.

'Guess what, mum? I'm in North Korea filming with the BBC – they're shooting tomorrow.' *16 April*

Thousands lined the route of Margaret Thatcher's cortege as it proceeded from the House of Commons through the streets of London to a lavish ceremonial funeral at St Paul's. Her husband Sir Denis Thatcher had died in 2003.

'Ah, Denis. Who was in charge up here – till now?' *17 April*

Communities Secretary Eric Pickles introduced a controversial proposal to allow people to build extensions to their properties, to a maximum of 26 feet into their gardens, without planning permission and without the need to consult their neighbours.

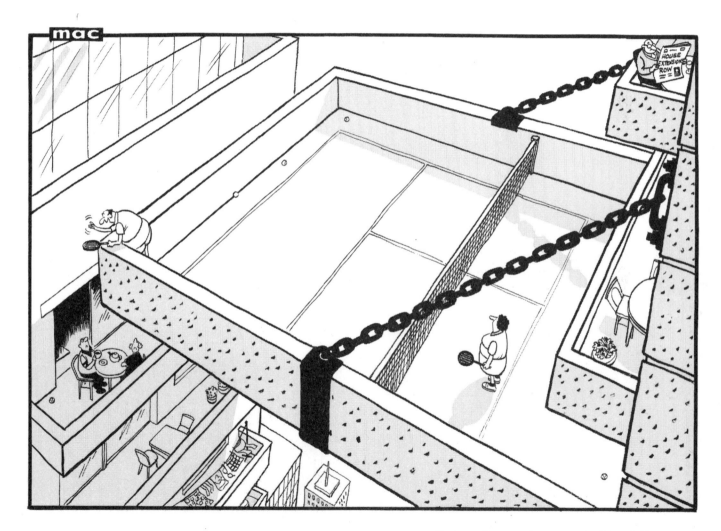

'Cooee. Can we have our ball back?' *19 April*

Liverpool FC striker Luis Suárez was fined and received a ten-game ban by the Football Association after he bit Chelsea's Bransilav Ivanovic during a match at Anfield.

'In my day top players would be in bed by now with a cup of cocoa.' *23 April*

Further concerns over cowboy cosmetic surgeons were aired in an official report by Sir Bruce Keogh, Medical Director of the NHS, who called for the introduction of new laws to protect patients.

'Ah, you've finished. How does she look with the bandages off?' *24 April*

A 57-year-old conman from Somerset, who sold fake bomb-detecting equipment based on novelty electronic golfball-finders, was sentenced to ten years in prison at the Old Bailey. Meanwhile, the European Court of Human Rights refused Britain's latest appeal to deport 'hate preacher' Abu Qatada to Jordan.

'That's it. I'm sure I saw mine twitch. The UK can't send Qatada back to Jordan.' *25 April*

David Cameron appointed Boris Johnson's 41-year-old brother Jo Johnson, MP for Orpington in Kent and a former *Financial Times* journalist, as the head of his Downing Street Policy Unit.

'Testing, testing... Hi, Jo. It's me, Boris... Coup d'état tomorrow at noon. Be ready...
Over and out.' *26 April*

Work and Pensions Secretary Iain Duncan Smith echoed earlier suggestions by Deputy Prime Minister Nick Clegg when he suggested that better-off pensioners should consider giving up some of their benefits, such as cold-weather payments, free television licences and free bus passes.

'We've decided to start using our bus passes. Would you direct us to the first-class compartment and bar?' *30 April*

Following a review of the 'holiday-camp culture' in jails ordered by Justice Secretary Chris Grayling, it was announced that a new 'Incentives and Earned Privileges' programme would be introduced in which prisoners would have to work or study to enjoy privileges such as satellite television sports channels.

'Keep going, Fingers. So far you've only earned the right to watch an early episode of *Teletubbies*.' *1 May*

In a surprising move, Tory grandee Lord Tebbit encouraged Conservatives to back the UK Independence Party in local elections where the Conservative candidate was unlikely to win. As Margaret Thatcher once famously said: 'You turn if you want to – the lady is not for turning.'

'UKIP if you want to – the lady is not for UKIPing!' *2 May*

After the spectacular local election success of UKIP (once called 'clowns' by the Conservatives' Kenneth Clarke) David Cameron promised to rush forward legislation for an 'in-out' referendum on Europe. However, many were disappointed when there was no mention of this in the Queen's Speech.

'Do I detect a tiny hint of protest planned for tomorrow's speech, dear?' *7 May*

Shortly before the State Opening of Parliament, Buckingham Palace announced that the Queen was to reduce her royal duties. Meanwhile, Dame Helen Mirren won an Olivier award for her role as the Queen in Peter Morgan's new play *The Audience* at the Gielgud Theatre in London.

'I'm sure that's Helen Mirren.' *8 May*

The retirement of popular, gum-chewing, 71-year-old Sir Alex Ferguson brought to an end his 27-year tenure as manager of Manchester United FC.

'We face ruin. Alex Ferguson has retired!' *9 May*

Justice Secretary Chris Grayling unveiled a new Offender Rehabilitation Bill, which aimed to turn short-term young offenders away from crime by employing 'mentors' who would help rehabilitate recently-released prisoners, and keep them under supervision for at least 12 months.

'Hello. Progress report on the Government's "mentor an ex-con for a year" scheme...
Day One...' *10 May*

After serving two months of his eight-month prison sentence for asking his ex-wife to take his speeding points, disgraced former Energy Secretary Chris Huhne was released from Leyhill Open Prison in Gloucestershire with an electronic tag and was photographed with his partner, Carina Trimingham.

'Chris has gone out. He asked me to wear his tag for him.' *14 May*

After intense pressure from mutinous Conservative Eurosceptics, David Cameron unveiled a EU Referendum Bill. Meanwhile, following riots outside previous international finance conferences, police began training with water cannon and body armour ahead of the G8 talks in Enniskillen, Northern Ireland.

'An all-out, no-holds-barred rebellion against Cameron's weak EU policy, you said – well go on, *REBEL!*' *15 May*

At the trial of seven men accused of operating a child sex ring in Oxford, an Old Bailey court heard of catastrophic failings by police and Oxfordshire County Council's social services department.

'Oh, very quiet. How has your day been?' *16 May*

The spectre of cloned babies was raised when scientists at a university in Oregon, USA, announced a breakthrough in human stem-cell research, using a technique which involved taking a sliver of skin from a patient's body.

'Go on. They took a sliver of your skin and put it into a test tube – then what?' *17 May*

In the wake of the gay marriage debate, the Government called for a consultation on the opening-up of civil partnerships to all, including heterosexuals, thereby giving tax advantages to nearly three million co-habiting unmarried couples in the UK.

'Would you like to come in for a cup of coffee, thereafter giving me all the tax advantages of a civil partnership?' *21 May*

A report by the UK Commission for Employment and Skills revealed that British workers are more stressed than at any time since records began more than 25 years ago. Meanwhile, it was revealed that GPs were struggling to cope with the knock-on effects of the closure of many hospital A&E departments.

'To be honest, doctor, I've queued for four hours to talk about *my* stress, not yours.' *22 May*

To help cope with the crisis in hospital A&E departments, NHS Confederation Chief Executive Mike Farrar, addressing a House of Commons Health Select Committee, suggested that GPs could be contacted by email to take the pressure off hospitals.

'Has the doctor replied to your email yet, mate?' *23 May*

In Woolwich, south London, close to the Royal Artillery Barracks, two Islamic extremists murdered a 25-year-old British soldier wearing a T-shirt with the logo of the army charity Help for Heroes emblazoned on it.

AN EVEN MORE UNITED KINGDOM *24 May*

It was revealed that a Dutch company was conducting trials in the USA of Lybrido, a new version of Viagra for women, which could be available to the public within three years.

'Your husband, Mrs Thompson? No, sorry, haven't seen him.' *28 May*

Environmental campaigners reacted with fury when Planning Minister Nick Boles said that building houses creates more human happiness than preserving fields, and unveiled plans to build 7,000 new homes on greenfield land in his constituency in Grantham, Lincolnshire.

'That was wonderful, darling. Did the earth move for you too?' *29 May*

A study by researchers at Imperial College London, which examined four million NHS operations in England between 2008 and 2011 in which patients spent at least one night in hospital, revealed that operations performed at weekends were less likely to be successful.

'Typical. It's the weekend, you're relaxing with friends in the pub, then some b*****d has to have an emergency operation!' *30 May*

In what many saw as a tax on village life itself, it was announced that expenses incurred in the running of amateur sports associations, such as cricket clubs, would be liable to taxation.

'Yes, it is a bit bumpy. That's where the taxman was standing when our heavy roller accidentally went over him.' *31 May*

In a speech made at Reuters' headquarters in London, Shadow Chancellor Ed Balls said that under a Labour government, 600,000 better-off pensioners would lose their winter fuel payments.

'Cover your ears. I have to break it to him that Labour are going to stop our winter fuel allowance.' *4 June*

Following the decision by the Home Office to relax the law banning the sale of alcohol at motorway service stations, J.D. Wetherspoon was granted a licence and planned to open its first pub on the M40 near Beaconsfield in Buckinghamshire.

'That's strange. I was told they were going to open a pub at this service station.' *5 June*

A damning report by the National Audit Office revealed that the BBC had spent £369 million on severance payments for its staff since 2005.

'Oh goody. Daddy must have been sacked by the BBC.' *2 July*

In Cairo, the Egyptian Army deposed the recently-elected President Mohamed Morsi. Meanwhile, Prince Charles (wearing a patched suit) visited the set of the BBC's *Doctor Who* TV series in Cardiff, to mark the 50th anniversary of the programme.

'Oh dear. A *coup d'état* in Egypt. Whatever next?' *5 July*

As the nation celebrated Andy Murray's victory at Wimbledon – the first British man to win the tennis championship since 1936 – it was revealed that 'hate preacher' Abu Qatada had finally been flown back to Jordan to face trial on terrorism charges after a legal battle to deport him from the UK that had lasted almost ten years.

'You're wasting your time, Abu. Even if you improve, the Brits aren't going to want you back!' *9 July*

There was an international media frenzy when the Duchess of Cambridge gave birth to an 8lb 6oz baby boy, Prince George Alexander Louis at St Mary's Hospital in London.

'It's so exciting. There's going to be photographic sessions, foreign dignitaries for the baby to meet, concerts, Morris dancers...' *23 July*